Table of Contents

Acknowledgments

I would like to express my gratitude to the many people who saw me through this book; to all those who provided support, talked things over, read, wrote, and offered comments—none of this could have been possible without any of you. Above all, I want to thank my family for the support. Thank you to those who supported and encouraged me despite all the time it took me away from you. It has been a long and difficult journey. Next, I would like to give thanks to Sandra Parsons, for without her assistance, this book would only have been a dream.

A special thanks to The Reentry Advocacy Project: Darwin Hamilton, Lewis Conway Jr, Charles Walker, Karen Keith, Lauren Johnson, and Reginald D. Smith for being an inspiration. I would also, like to acknowledge all the men and women coming home from prison. This book is written in your honor, to shed the light on the barriers and struggles we go through.

Introduction

At the end of 2015, there was more than two million prisoners in the United States being held in state or federal correctional facilities.[1] Every year, thousands of people are released from jail or prison. Most incarcerated people will eventu-ally be released, but majority of these individuals will return to a life of freedom without the nec-essary skills they need to survive. Recidivism rates suggest that many of these individuals will reoffend within six months of release, and most will reoffend within three years.[2]

This is not because they're bad people; it's because they are trying to thrive in a system that sets them up to fail. Given grim post-re-lease arrest rates, it's hard to understand why our government is not doing more to help those transitioning from incarceration to life on the outside. It doesn't make sense for taxpayer dol-lars to go towards incarcerating people over and over— it seems that the money could be better

---

1   (Carson & Anderson, 2016)

2   (Durose, Cooper and Snyder 2014)

spent improving rehabilitation programs for inmates as well as in other positive area such as reentry programs.

Increased funding for programs aimed at help-ing formerly incarcerated transition to life on the outside would likely lead to better outcomes for those individuals, fewer crimes being committed, and lower recidivism rates. One would hope that our society would want to see people who are incarcerated serve their time, get rehabilitated, be released, and become productive members of their communities.

It is well known that formerly incarcerated people face significant challenges upon being released. Some of these challenges include bar-riers to obtaining employment, difficulty finding housing, difficulty accessing education, mental health issues, substance abuse, stigma, and social isolation. These challenges can make transitioning from a life of incarceration to a life of freedom extremely difficult, especially if the person has been incarcerated for a long time.

In our rapidly changing world, it is reasonable to expect that in addition to the challenges mention, those who have been incarcerated for a long time probably also struggle to adapt to the significant changes that took place while they were on the inside. Although people in prison are there because they have committed a crime, they deserve the opportunity to re-enter life on the outside after serving their sentence with half of a fighting chance. Those in custody should have the opportunity to participate in training courses that will enable them to successfully transition into society.

They should have access to employment training such as the tools and skills needed to be successful. Also, life skills training, adult education, mental health services and other programs that target their needs will maximize their likelihood of success after release. The process of planning a prisoner's journey back into the world should start on the day they go through the prison gates. Providing inmates with the opportunity to rehabilitate, put their pasts behind them, and start fresh should be a priority of the justice system, and for society.

I take this position from a perspective of compassion for fellow human beings, but also from an economic perspective. Investing in rehabilitation and reentry programs for inmates has a great positive impact on our lives, but it also benefits society. Lower recidivism rates mean fewer crimes (at least fewer crimes committed by former inmates), and reduced prison populations. The cost of maintaining prisons is huge. A focus on rehabilitation programs would mean better employment and housing outcomes for former inmates, which would mean less long-term use of social assistance programs.

The majority of individuals who are incarcerated are not serving life sentences and will one day be returning to a life on the outside. These individuals deserve our justice system's best efforts toward rehabilitation. Once a person has done their time they should be able to return home with a clean slate. The opportunity to acquire skills that will allow them to be successful upon release is key but having these opportunities on the inside is only part of the equation.

It is also important that reentry programs extend through the period of transition that occurs upon release. This can be achieved by establishing relationships between prison rehabilitation programs and relevant community partners.

Once released, formerly incarcerated people face significant challenges. They will head to halfway houses and supervised release programs. It is important that their reentry pro-grams continue into these environments. This can be facilitated by coordination and collabo-ration between key staff members from prison rehabilitation programs and supervised release programs. Reintegrating back into society is not something that will happen overnight. It is a lengthy process that can be very challenging, and very trying. It is also a process that requires ongoing work, and ongoing support.

Formerly incarcerated inmates are somewhat doomed to face a lifetime of barriers because of past convictions. Many of these individuals want to do good in the world, and have worked hard to turn their lives around, yet these barriers still haunt them. It is important to have reentry programs in place that address the barriers that can be crippling to former inmates. How can someone do right when there are so many barriers standing in their way?

We as a nation can do better. These individuals are suffering because of broken policies that are designed to keep us in the system forever. Providing these individuals with much needed training and support can be critical. Helping them develop life skills and coping skills is important. Helping them to find jobs after release is important. We need to help them to build their morals and keep them on the right path. Speaking as a person who has been down this road, the challenges can be very debilitating, and at times, you may want to give up. I hope that you won't.

In this book, I will discuss the significant challenges that formerly incarcerated individuals face on the road to reentry, and some resources that may be helpful. If you have served time and are now struggling to reintegrate into life on the out-side, this book is for you. Maybe you can draw some inspiration or hope from this book. If you have a friend or loved one who was recently released or will soon be released, perhaps this book can give you an idea about the types of challenges that lie ahead for them, and how you can help. If you don't really have a connection to incarceration in anyway?

Well, I'm glad you're here. Maybe some of information you will read in this book makes you question our justice system's status quo. Maybe it will make you reconsider how you think about people who have spent time in jail or prison. Maybe it will change the way you think about second chances.

Chapter One

Many formerly incarcerated individuals want to live as law-abiding citizens. We want to do normal things, like get a job, find a decent apart-ment, make some friends, and be productive members of society. These might not sound like difficult things, but people with a history of incarceration will face limited opportunities because of our past. It's very hard for those released from prison with no one to turn to, or nowhere to go. If it wasn't for shelters, many would have no were to go other than the streets.

Those returning to their own homes are lucky, but many may have lost their former accommodations when they went into custody. Some are lucky to have the help of friends or family, but most want to be able to support themselves. To do that, they need to find work and try to further their education. In this chapter, I'll discuss the barriers to find work once being released from prison and offer some strategies that might be helpful when starting out. Many individuals who are released from prison are released on parole.

Parole allows someone convicted of a crime to serve the last portion of their sentence under the supervision of a parole officer. This way they wouldn't have to finish their sentence in prison. Parole is only granted under certain conditions. The purpose behind this is to help people that are believed to be unlikely to reoffend. Conditions of parole are rules that a parolee must abide by. Failure to abide by those rules could result in them being returned to prison to serve out their time.

One of the conditions of parole is that parolees must go out and find a job. However, this is easier said than done, because having a criminal record makes it difficult to find work. It's easy to put guidelines in place saying that parolees need to secure jobs, but when employers won't hire people with criminal records, it becomes challenging to comply with the conditions of parole. Don't get me wrong, there are some good employment opportunities out there for parolees and formerly incarcerated individuals.

There are organizations that are willing to hire people with a criminal record. But there are also many that are not. The sad truth is that many organizations have policies in place that prevent them from hiring anyone with a felony conviction. Some have policies that prevent them from hiring anyone with a criminal record. Many former inmates face significant challenges find-ing work upon release and dealing with various kinds of stigma and shame.

What happens when an individual is not successful in finding work? Those with limited income and nothing to give their lives structure often go back to breaking the law. When a formerly incarcerated person learns that an employer is not willing to give them a chance, they can become discouraged. It's hard to move on from your past when you're not given the chance to redeem yourself, and a person coming out of prison is not always given a fair chance. I believe that everyone should be given a chance to prove themselves as a valuable employee.

No, it's not impossible to find a job when you have a criminal record, but it is challenging. If you do find a job, it's hard to find one where you will be given a fair opportunity. The challenges associated with being released and looking for work are not just the practical ones, but also the mental ones. Having to adjust to a new routine is not easy. Or, for some, the absence of a routine may be hard to adjust to. Without some job skills and job search training, many formerly incarcerated individuals will not be successful in finding work.

Many people are leaving prison with limited education and limited work history, and that alone makes it difficult to get hired. Pair that with a criminal record—it's quite the barrier indeed. Although they may not come out and say it, employers are unlikely to hire formerly incarcerated individuals because they view them as a liability. Some may worry about theft while others may worry about being sued for damages resulting from their negligent hiring, and some may worry about loss of sales due customers perceptions.

Companies are willing to consider hiring an individual—if they have only been convicted of a nonviolent crime. Most people leaving jail or prison are not looking to return. Many want to defy the odds and build a successful life, but it's not easy to do it when they are struggling to find employment opportunities.

The struggle for these individuals is real. It can be easy to lose hope and start to believe that they'll never get ahead. Those with a rocky his-tory often find it hard to leave their past in the past. After failed attempt upon failed attempt at "going legit," they may start to believe that their only option is to return to their old lifestyle—the one that landed them in prison in the first place. These individuals quickly realize not everybody is willing to give someone fresh out a second chance. Not everyone is willing to look past the conviction and consider the skills you may have.

Even on parole, it can still feel like you are doing time. No matter what you try to do to get ahead, it seems your past stays to haunt you. The rest of your life you will be labeled as a felon, a criminal, or an ex -con. Even if you were convicted a long time ago, your record will follow you throughout your life. You might dream about how much easier life would be if you didn't have that shadow hanging over your head.

Without doubt, it is a struggle. This is not to say that it is impossible to find a job and get back on your feet. You can do it, but fair warning: it's not going to be easy. It's one of those things that take a lot of hard-work and perseverance. It requires being willing to adopt a new lifestyle and being steadfast in the face of uncertainty and discouragement. To be honest, it means heaving to accept things that are not fair at times. Having a second chance at life means working on yourself and becoming a better person.

Anything is possible if you are willing to put in the hard-work. It's not something that will happen overnight, and it's not something that you can do by yourself. You need to be willing to reach out to others, make connections, and not stop until you succeed. Many individuals will find their first employment opportunities post-release through temp agencies or at Good-will. Temp agencies help people looking for work connect with employers who are looking to fill temporary short-term positions.

These types of arrangements may not seem ideal, but they give you a chance to make some money and gain some work experience. Once you have valuable work experience under your belt, you can secure new opportunities. It's better to start somewhere than to remain broke and unemployed.

Some individuals have luck with small locally owned companies, as they may be more willing to hear you out. These companies have no HR departments or middlemen. With these business, your likely to get an opportunity to talk with the owner and explain yourself. When a business owner sees you as a person rather than a policy, you have a greater chance of being hired, or at least making a connection. Even if they don't end up hiring you, they may be able to point you in the right the direction.

Meeting potential employers and networking in the community can feel daunting, but it can be a valuable source of employment leads. Everyone knows a word of mouth alone can lead to new opportunities. Maybe the first employer you meet with doesn't have any openings, but he mentions that his friend is looking for someone. Maybe the friend just filled the position, but they take your contact information and pass it along to a contact of who is hiring. For this reason, it's a clever idea to have some basic business cards printed. All they need to include is your name and contact information.

That way, if you meet a potential employer, or someone who might know a potential employer, you can pass along your card and say that you'd love to any discuss opportunities. If you don't know how to get business cards, try visiting a supply store such as Office Max, Staples and so on, or just ask your parole officer, case man-ager, or anyone who is helping you transition. If you don't have anyone, check the phone book or online to see if there is an employment help center in your area, they should be able to help. It's also a great idea to try to get contact information for potential employers that you chat with.

Even if they don't have anything right now, you can drop them a line thanking them for meeting with you. This will keep you fresh in their minds and show that you appreciated their time. Once you have their contact information, nothing is stopping you from following up with them in a month or two to see if anything has changed. When you are fresh out of prison, life may seem hard. But treating your job search like a job is a good approach, for a couple of reasons.

One, if you spend eight hours a day actively looking for work, you are much more likely to find work than if you spend only an hour a day. It only makes sense. Two, getting into the habit of spending eight hours a day working at some-thing is great preparation for when you land a job. It can be hard to stay positive, but the key is not to let your past become your future, and not to let old mistakes keep you down. It is what it is. Pick up the pieces and keep on moving forward. Make the best out of being free. Going to bed at decent time and waking up early will help to train your body. Not only that, it will give you a sense of dignity and a purpose. When you finally land a job, a schedule won't be a problem.

Throughout your job search, keep in mind that certain industries might be more willing to hire former inmates than others. As previously mentioned, small businesses are a good bet, and staffing agencies might be a suitable place to start. If you set your hopes on getting an office job and company car, that's not likely to happen right away. Labor-type jobs in industries like construction, landscaping, roofing, manufacturing, and packing seem to be the most lenient. These may not be best jobs in the world, but they will give you much needed experience. Be willing to accept any job, if it's safe, and the employer is willing to give you the chance you deserve. Finding a job is not easy, but it's not impossible, either.

You just got to be willing to do research and get out and look in the right places. If you have a Parole Officer who is helping you transition into your new life, ask them for help. Use every opportunity available to you! Each person leaving prison is an individual with different strengths and abilities. There are many factors that come into play when searching for a job. Some of these factors are length of time since last conviction, type of conviction, time incarcerated, age, previous work experience, attitude, and skill. These are just the things pertaining to you.

Other factors beyond your control include the economic climate, the job market, etc. The list goes on and on, so don't get down when you get turned down for a job. There are other opportunities out there, so stick with it. If you are successful in landing a job, there are two main things you must keep: a good attitude and a decent work ethic. The one thing you must realize is that it will take some challenging work and energy, and at times you will get discouraged. When all else fails, you should keep faith in yourself and fight for what you want.

Chapter Two

We know that every day, hundreds of people are released from prison or jail. And we've started to get an idea of some of the struggles they face. One of the struggles that present itself immediately upon release is the question of housing. Where is a freshly released man or woman to go? Some have family or friends waiting for them on the outside, but some are not so lucky. So where do formerly incarcerated people go once they have been released? Some are assigned to a halfway house as part of their release.

A halfway house is an institution that provides the formerly incarcerated a place to live with others, while learning the skills they need to reintegrate into society. The purpose of the halfway house is to offer the support and resources required to help the individual successfully transition, and hope-fully reduce the likelihood of recidivism. Some may be fortunate enough to have a release plan in place that involves working with a social worker that can help them secure housing through social assistance or community programs.

Having someone to advocate for his or her needs can be very beneficial for someone trying to reenter society. However, not everyone who is released from prison or jail gets assigned to a halfway house, and not everyone has a good caseworker supporting them.

Many are left to fend for themselves. These people are at significant risk, because in the absence of friends or family to put them up during this time, they basically have two options: a homeless shelter, or the streets. But wait, you might be thinking, couldn't they look for an apartment like everyone else? The answer is no because most places do background checks.

Well, they can try, but most will become quickly discouraged. Looking for an apartment when you have a criminal record it's very complicated, time consuming, and a disheartening endeavor. Most people who are released from prison or jail want to get back on their feet and make decent lives for themselves. Doing that becomes very difficult when you realize that you may have no place to live. Obviously, there are financial barriers – many people just getting released have no income, no job, and no savings. But even if money were not a pressing concern, the fact is that many landlords refuse to rent to anyone with a criminal record. This may be true regard-less of the nature of the conviction, or the length of time since the conviction.

If you think that sounds like discrimination, you're right. However, there is currently no explicit law in the United States preventing landlords from refusing to rent based on criminal records alone. The Fair Housing Act forbids discrimination based on race, color, national origin, religion, sex, familial status or handicap.[3] Notice there's no mention of criminal record, incarceration, arrest, or felon status. These days, almost every application you fill out includes the question "Have you ever been convicted of a felony?"

Landlords may have one or more of several reasons for refusing the rent to people with a criminal record. One reason is that in some sit-auctions, landlords may be held liable for the actions of their tenants, so they view renting to someone with a criminal record as exposing themselves to risk. They may also believe that someone with a criminal record is more likely to cause costly damages to the property. Another reason, especially in the context of rental prop-arty complexes like apartment buildings, is perceptions of other renters.

There are many people who would be fearful of living in the same apartment building as someone who has been to jail or prison. These people are thinking about their safety and the safety of their families, but they are not considering that many convictions are of a non-violent nature. They are also not considering that many people who have served time are not interested in returning to a criminal lifestyle. They only want to be law-abiding citizens while trying to rebuild their lives. From a business perspective, property management companies may believe that renting to someone with a criminal record will result in tenants moving out or prospective tenants being turned off from the building.

3. (U.S. Department of Housing and Urban Development, 2017)

When this happens, it can result in decreased demand and lower property values. Therefore, many of landlords have a tenant screening process that includes a criminal background check. For this reason, it is very likely that a former inmate will be rejected when trying to find housing through property management companies. The barriers to obtaining safe and secure housing pose significant risk for vulnerable people just being released.

During this time, post-release support is critical because it may form their expectations for their life on the outside. If someone serves their time and is released from prison or jail ready to work hard at getting their life back on track, they can become very discouraged when they are receiving rejection after rejection. With nowhere to go, they might turn to the streets. Or, they might turn to the people who were in their social circles before they were incarcerated. Chances are these people may not be the best influence on our recently returned citizens.

When a person with a criminal record is forced to live on the streets or forced to associate with people who are still involved in crime, there is a very real chance that they may end up returning to their old ways. Not because they want to, but to many of them, it's their only chance at survival. If you've never been involved in crime, or been close to anyone who has, it might be hard for you to imagine how a person gets into a situation where they return to a life of crime after serving time.

Most people who have served time have no interest in going back to prison. But the barriers to reintegrating to life on the outside make it seem impossible to survive without breaking the law. When a person cannot find housing because every place they try runs a background check, what are they to do? When they can't find a legitimate job, for the same reason, what options do they have? Essentially, they have neither somewhere to live, nor a reliable income.

Yes, they may be able to stay in a homeless shelter for a while, but that is not a permanent solution. Yes, some may be eligible for social assistance and may get a small amount of money that way, but it is not enough to survive on. In fact, many don't even have these options.

For years, our government has imposed laws and policies that work against people leaving prison. Over the past twenty years, many states in America have limited or denied access to social assistance programs for those with drug felony charges. Such as the SNAP program and public housing.

This is a political approach to the "war on drugs" that raged in the US in the late 90s and early 2000s in response to an increase in drug-related crime. Although these policies were put in place to help prevent social assistance dollars being used to fund drug habits and drug crimes, they may have done more harm than good. There are three federally funded housing assistance programs in America that aim to provide afford-able housing to people with low-incomes: The Public Housing Program, the Section 8 Housing Choice Voucher program, and the Section 8 rental assistance program.[4] Although

4   (McCarty, Falk, Aussenberg, & Carpenter, 2016)

these are federal programs, they are administered in each state by public housing authorities, each having flexibility in determining eligibility criteria.

According to federal law, public housing author-ties are required to deny eligibility to anyone with a lifetime registration as a sex offender. Two of these programs, the Public Housing Pro-gram and the Section 8 Housing Program, are also required to deny eligibility to anyone who has been convicted of producing methamphetamine-amines on the premises of assisting housing units. These are two very specific exclusionary criteria, but public housing authorities have freedom to develop their own entry requirements, which may include any felony convictions.

With limited access the public housing, and with many property management companies refusing to rent to people with records, formerly incarcerated people will almost certainly face significant barriers to obtaining housing. For many, public housing is their only hope of find-ing a safe and stable place to live. With no secure place to call their own, no job to keep them busy, and no legitimate way of earning income for food, clothing, etc., a person needs to look for other options. Unfortunately, many of those other options involve illegal activities.

It is heartbreaking to see the way the current norms and policies in our society are preventing former inmates from rebuilding their lives, and sometimes forcing them back in the life of crime they so desperately want to leave behind. If the government really wanted people with felony drug convictions to go legit, they wouldn't place people in circumstances that prevent them from accomplishing their goals. If a person with a drug charge can't get social assistance, can't find a job, can't get public housing, and is turned away by private landlords, then how in the world are they supposed to survive?

If they turn back to selling drugs, it's because they believed there was no other choice. This is not a system that wants to rehabilitate former inmates, but insure they return to crime. One that does not want to see these people rebuild their lives and go legit. It is a system designed to keep them down, to ensure they end up back in prison. It's not fair to the men and women who served their time and deserve another chance, and it's not fair to the tax payers whose money is tied up funding prisons.

America has been reluctant to embrace the fact that everyone deserves to have a decent place to live. Some would go as far to say that public housing is not a right. The fact is if you have a felony conviction then you will have a tough time finding housing. From a personal perspective, I have been through these issues myself and at times I wanted to give up. But I knew that I didn't want to be back in jail or prison again.

Although it's still hard for me thirteen years later and I'm still dependent on someone else for shelter. How can a person get ahead when road-blocks continue to get in their way? Every day, I wonder what could've been if I hadn't gone down the wrong path. One mistake can have such a detrimental impact on your life. In the case of a criminal conviction, no matter how minor the crime is, you may pay for your mistake for years to come. Every day is a challenge, but I do my best to accept the things I cannot change and work hard to change the things I can.

Just because a person makes a mistake, doesn't mean that they will make it again. Some people do learn their lesson the first time. So why are so many people leaving prison still being denied help? These people need help. Getting back on their feet is not easy, and without support, they might fail. I have known many individuals who meant well and wanted so badly to live right. But the barriers and roadblocks forced them back into the criminal lifestyle. Even after prison, it feels like we are doing time. Why should a person who has served their time be forced to pay for their mistake again and again?

Trying to put your past behind you is a long-term struggle, and people transitioning from prison to the outside world need support. America is in dire need of more prerelease centers. Prerelease centers are facilities that house inmates for a designated time leading up to their scheduled release. They focus on easing the transition into the outside world by helping inmates develop employment skills, access healthcare, access housing, and build relation-ships within their communities.

These centers increase an inmates' chance of successful transition and take the burden off homeless shelters and half ways houses. Pre-release centers are ideal because they specialize in addressing the specific needs of people leaving prison. Although many inmates face similar struggles when they are released (barriers to accessing housing and employment, social isolation, etc.), no two people are the same. Prerelease centers may be able to offer supports tailored to the individual. Staying at a prerelease center also gives those who don't have anywhere to go time to sort things out.

This reduces their vulnerability and reduces the likelihood that they will fall back into old ways. Certainly, the first step in rebuilding a life on the outside is to genuinely want to change. But that isn't enough. Even the most dedicated need a support system in place. If you are a for-merely incarcerated individual, no matter what you do, it will always be hard to find your place. You will face significant barriers, including a system that generally sets you up to fail. We deserve better. We need to pull together and make our voices heard, from the steps of the Capitol to the steps of Capitol Hill.

Making changes is not easy; it takes hard-work and dedication. We must stay determined not to let our pasts become our future. All Americans have a right to freedom, including those who have served their time. The only way to bring about change is to fight for it. Opportunities are not going to be plentiful, so you must get out there and work hard for what you want. Everything that comes easy is not always good for you. Something could hinder you. Yes, you will experience rejection and setbacks, but you can't let it take you off the path to reentry. Learn to use the troubled times as motivation to do better. Just keep in mind the hardest things you went through, and the good things you are trying to achieve. The bad has passed, and now it time to look forward to the good.

When trying to stay out of trouble, you must stay away from trouble. That means keeping away from the negative influence of the friends you associated with leading up to your incarceration. Now, if those friends are also working to rebuild their lives, you could be a reliable source of support for each other. I'm referring to the people who are still living the old lifestyle—the lifestyle that got you locked up. You need to stay away from that.

Having a safe and stable place to live means that you won't be out on the streets where you might run into some of those dangerous people such as those you were prior friends with. If you have access to any kind of support, whether it is a parole officer, a prerelease center, a case-worker, or even a community center, try your best to seek help finding housing.

If you are eligible for public housing pursue it. I know you may not have the luxury of any of those things. If that is the case, and if you don't have anyone you can stay with, you can try to seek a rental agreement with a private landlord. For example, maybe someone is renting a room in their house to get some help with the rent or mortgage. Maybe you can try a faith-based group home or boarding house.

Renting a room is usually much cheaper than renting an entire apartment, so it may be a good option. Additionally, private landlords often vet their own tenants and don't do comprehensive background checks. They may not ask about your criminal record, whereas a property man-agement company most likely will. If you do secure a place to live, you want to keep busy. Keeping busy means you don't have time to get into trouble! If you can find a job, that's wonderful. Or maybe you're interested in increasing your education before you enter the workforce?

That's a great option, too. If you're lucky enough to have a caseworker, a parole officer, or the support of a prerelease center, they can help you explore your options for education. Even if you don't have any of these support structures in place, there might be some support available at your local community center.

Even if you can't get funding for formal education, there may be life skills class you can take, or even a hobby you can work on by yourself. Developing yourself, whatever it takes, will help you carve out a purpose in your new life. This might sound harsh, but if you are not willing or ready to change, you may as well reserve a space in prison, because most likely, you will be back.

If you are ready to change, the first few months out will be critical. Being judged for your past is part of reentry, and you will have to deal with that, unfair as it is. Some people will see is your record. Some people will think that you can't do anything else. I can't say this enough: you must prove them wrong. We must prove to them that we can change and that we are worthy.

Sometimes you must remain humble and let your actions speak for themselves. You will be dealing with stigma, and it's not an easy thing to experience. It's easy to become discouraged, or to get so angry that you lash out, but you need to stay focused and use your energy to be the best version of yourself that you can be. No

one ever said that the road back would be easy. Fighting for what you want—actually, fighting for what you need—is an uphill battle, and it doesn't seem fair because it's not. But you and I both know this is the country we live in. Yes, it's easy to become bitter (most people would). However, try to stay grateful for your freedom and use it to do what you can to make your life better. It's a fact, that people will look at you differently once you get out. That is something
you should expect.

You will run across people that will be rude and cruel to you. Some will dismiss you and it will hurts. You should know, it says more about them than it does about you. Although there are so many ignorant people out there, you will also meet some good ones. Don't be afraid to ask for help. You are going to need it, and I believe you deserve it. It's better to ask for help and keep your freedom, then to keep your pride and end up back in prison.

Always try to take what you can get until something better comes along. I spent my first year out working odd jobs at the labor hall. It wasn't something I wanted to do, but I did what I had to do to earn money and stay free. At the end of the day money is money and it all spends the same. Long as the work is safe, I say take any job you can get. Sometimes you must start at the bottom and work your way up. No one can be successful overnight—it takes time and dedication. The same goes for housing.

Maybe the first place you get is not your dream home. Maybe it's a tiny bedroom with a shared kitchen and bathroom. But if it's a safe place to live, it's 100% better than the streets. At your first job, be a model employee. With your first rental agreement, be a model tenant. Build a relationship with your employer and your land-lord. Then, when you're ready to move on, you can ask those people for reference letters. Having good references will strengthen your next job application and give future landlords confidence.

One of the best things I ever did was ask for help—the extra support helped me find my footing. Sometimes when you think you have no options left, you make that connection that can help you over the biggest hurdle. Asking for help is one of the hardest things about living on the outside. It's humbling, and it's uncomfortable, and it makes us vulnerable. But you know what? Rebuilding your life is going to be as humbling as it is uncomfortable. It's also going to be worth it.

Chapter Three

It's hard starting over once you get out, but it can be done if you want it. It will take a strong will and lots of motivation, but anything is possible if you are committed. You may feel excited and anxious to get things underway, but it is important to remember to take it one day at time. Remember, God didn't create earth in one day— even he needed six days. So, it might take you a little while, and that's OK. The first few months out is going to be your time to adjust but don't be afraid to go out and meet new people. Find folks that share some of your interests. Go and enjoy yourself, maybe pick up a new hobby.

Go fishing, take a walk by the lake, anything that will keep you engaged and motivated. In addition to the struggles of finding work and finding stable housing, many formerly incarcerated people transitioning back into society struggle with social isolation. Past behavior may have caused them to become estranged from family and old friends. This can be extremely painful. They are likely struggling with feelings of guilt and shame and may be embarrassed or afraid to face their families. The friends you spent time with before prison is more likely still involved in crime and should be avoided.

It's very important for newly released man or woman to avoid negative influences from their past. Human beings are social animals, and most of us become unhappy when we spend prolonged periods of time alone. The feeling of isolation that many former inmates experience extends beyond the state of being physically alone. It also stems from the sense of stigma and shame that many formerly incarcerated carries with them. It makes us feel like we don't have a place in society.

These feelings of shame may come from within, but the judgement and discrimination former inmates face upon their release also reinforces them. Dealing with these feelings is not a simple undertaking. Finding a way to forgive oneself for past mistakes is part of it and making connections and joining the outside world is another part. These things are easier said than done, and the emotional journey to reentry is often long and difficult. Everybody needs somebody. Sometimes the supportive types of relationships are so important for a former inmate that starting over is hard to achieve. It is important to make friends with people who are living right, rather than falling in with a crowd who are not living right.

Friends are an important source of support and inspiration. Yeah, you might think that it's going to be hard to make friends once people find out about your record, but there are lots of people in the world who believe in second chances. A wonderful way to meet likeminded people is to get involved in community activities. For example, if you enjoy sports, there might be some intra-mural sports available at your local community center. You can probably get a free pass for a few visits to see if you like it, and you might meet some great people. If you can't afford to do any activities that will cost you extra money, there are probably free things you can get involved in, like walking groups, or a book club at the library. Volunteer activities are also a great (free) way to meet people. And who knows? You might find helping someone out to be extremely rewarding.

Another source of companionship and inspiration might be a support group for former inmates. If you have access to the Internet (try your local library), you can likely get connected with such a group. Better yet, if you stayed in a pre-release center, you are probably already connected with a group. Memberships in groups like these are free, and usually consists of regular group meetings where people share their experiences, struggles, and successes with living life on the outside. You can learn a lot from other people who have been out a bit longer.

They may have some tips to share about how they overcame the struggles during those first few months. If you live in a small town, there may not be a local group like this. But online, there is a group for absolutely everything. If you can get Internet access for an hour a week, you can connect with formerly incarcerated individuals or support groups online. It's important to realize that the way you survived on the inside is different from the way you must survive now that you're free. While in prison, you might have had to form alliances with some bad people to ensure your safety.

Depending on how long you were inside, those experiences probably have a big effect on how you view relationships with others. You might find it very hard to trust others. That's normal. You might find the entire process of trying to make friends very overwhelming. It's OK to ease yourself into things, but do not isolate yourself.

This is not to say that everyone you knew in prison is a bad person. Maybe you had friends on the inside who are out now and are also struggling to rebuild their lives. If that's the case, it's great to stay in touch and support each other. Be sure to look out for each other, and don't let one another fall back into their old ways. If one of your friends does get sucked back in, you can try to help him, but not at the risk of your own well-being and freedom. Just know when to draw the line before it is too late.

At the end of the day, everybody wins when a person stays out of prison and gets their life on track. With the will to do right and a dedicated support system, you will survive. The road is filled with many obstacles, but you can't let them steer you off course. Only the strong will survive this difficult transition. Are you one of the strong! You might not believe that but look at it this way: if you can survive prison, anything is possible. Try your best to get some supportive people in your corner, and you will slowly find yourself growing into your new life. The one thing I learned is not to take no for an answer.

If you get one no, or two, or three, keep trying until you get that yes. Hearing no is better than hearing the prison door close behind you. Yes, it's going to be hard, but it won't be as difficult as doing hard time. I know the struggle. I've been there, and I know what it's like to jump hurdles after hurdles and face repeated rejection.

If rebuilding your life was easy, everybody would be doing it, and prisons would be half full. You should decide if you are willing to put in the work or give up. The choice is yours, but you know the result if you choose the easy way out. Crime does not pay. At some point, you get tired of the life of crime. We need more people getting out and doing right to help reduce these barriers. Going from a number to a name is a big deal.

Life on the inside and the outside both have struggles, it's just that the struggles are differ-ent. On the outside, you have the freedom to decide how to handle them. It will take a lot of work to adjust to a new lifestyle. Many of those coming home will need to put in a lot of work and get a lot of support to make it. That's why it is important to find a support group once you are released.

You are going to learn an unusual way of approaching friendship and trust. Hopefully a healthier way. When you were serving time, you likely felt isolated, and as a result, you might be used to trying to do everything on your own. Combating social isolation and learning how to have healthy relationships is one of those things that you simply cannot do by yourself. So, do your best to let someone in.

You have so much to adjust to once you're free, it can be overwhelming. That's one reason it is important not to isolate yourself. You may not have much faith in people, depending what kind of relationships you had on the inside, but it's important to put yourself out there. Making friends will be easier than you think. You must stay humble through it all and believe that everyone in this world has room to grow.

Being free means that you get to direct your own growth and make your own choices. It's a big responsibility, but it beats the hell out of being locked in a cage. Nobody lives forever, so why not put in the work and enjoy your hard-earned freedom. You've been given the opportunity to have a second chance; don't let it get away. Be the best that you can be. Don't be afraid to take chances that are going to be life changing. Make sure that the chances you're taking are the right chances.

Chapter Four

Since deinstitutionalization occurred in the
1970s, the number of people with mental illness in
U.S. prisons and jails has dramatically risen. The
dismal conditions of many of these facilities, paired
with the lack of mental health services available,
mean that many of these inmates will experience a
deterioration of their mental health while serving
their time. Not surprisingly, this will put them at a
serious disadvantage when they tackle the
complicated process of trying to rein-tegrate into
society upon their release. It's hard to talk about
incarceration and reentry, and the experiences that
go with them, without talking about mental health.

Formerly incarcerated people reintegrating into
society upon release face challenges that are so
complex, multi-layered, and interconnected that
it's hard to wrap our heads around them. It's even
harder to break them down into chapters so that
we can use this book as a medium to discuss
them. People being released from jail or prison are
vulnerable to homelessness, unemployment,

social isolation, mental illness, substance abuse, stigma, shame, and a host of other negative experience that put them at a disadvantage. The thing is, these things are not independent from one another.

The barriers to obtaining employment and secure housing, for example, are not only caused by discrimination based on presence of a criminal record. Having no job means having no money for a phone, which means being hard to reach, which makes it hard to get calls about employment opportunities. Having no phone also makes it difficult to apply for a job—it doesn't look very good when an applicant can't give a hiring manager a contact number.

Not having a stable place to live means a person may not have all their things in one place, and may not look put together, which means it's harder to make a good first impression with an employer. Having a mental illness exacerbates social isolation, which make it difficult to net-work to find a job or socialize to make friends. It might mean that some days, a person is so unwell that they cannot accomplish any of the goals they have set for themselves. If they are successful in landing a job, their mental illness might interfere.

For example, they might have bad days on which they are unable to work. Or if they are in treatment, they may have to miss work for appointments. Missing work does not look good to an employer, especially early in the employment relationship. This makes it harder to keep a job, which increases the chance of homelessness. Being unemployed and/or homeless puts former inmates at risk of falling back into their old lifestyles. Clearly, mental health is a crucial factor in successful reentry. Even outside the context of reentry, mental health is a huge issue in our country. In 2015, the Substance Abuse and Mental Health Ser-vices Administration (SAMHSA) conducted the National Survey on Drug Use and Health. Results suggest that an estimated 43.4 million non-institutionalized adults in America experienced some type of mental illness during the past year.[5] "Some type" of mental illness means any mental, emotional, or behavioral disorder that met diagnostic criteria as defined in the Diagnostic and Statistical Manual of Mental Disorders, 4th Edition (DSM-IV), excluding developmental disorders and substance use disorders.[6] This 43.4 million represents 17.9% of all adults in America. Of those 43.4 million, 9.8 million had what the SAMHSA calls a "serious mental illness." That is, one that significantly interferes with at least one major life activity While these numbers might be startling, what is even more alarming is that only 43.1% of the 43.4 million who had a mental illness received mental health care services during the past year. To be clear, these results suggest that fewer than half of all people who had a mental illness got the help they needed. [7]

The same survey revealed that an estimated 20.8 million people (7.8% of Americans) age 12 and over experienced a substance use disorder

---

5   (Center for Behavioral Health Statistics and Quality, 2016)
6   (Center for Behavioral Health Statistics and Quality, 2016)
7   (Center for Behavioral Health Statistics and Quality, 2016)

(SUD) in the past year. The most common SUD was alcohol use disorder, experienced by 15.7 million people. An additional 7.7 million people experienced illicit drug use disorder. As might be expected, there was some overlap, with 2.7 million people experiencing both alcohol and illicit drug use disorder in the past year. [8]

Some of these people may have sought help from other sources, such as community groups or 12 step programs, but only a very small proportion received help from a specialized source. These numbers suggest that mental illness and substance abuse are struggles faced by a significant portion of the population, and that fewer than half are getting the treatment they need. The reasons for not seeking treatment are numerous and complex but need to include stigma associated with mental illness and barriers to accessing healthcare. So, if these are the numbers for the general population, what are the stats among inmates? You probably will not be surprised to learn that they are even more grim. There is some variability in the literature regarding the prevalence of mental illness among inmates, but most studies show that the rates are higher among inmates than among the genearl population.[9] Two major surveys conducted by the Bureau of Justice Statistics, The Survey of Inmates in State and Correctional Facilities (2004)[10], and the Survey of Inmates in Local Jails (2002)[11] are frequently cited.

8   (Center for Behavioral Health Statistics and Quality, 2016)
9   (Prins, 2014)
10   (Bueau of Justice Statistics, 2004)
11   (Bureau of Justice Statistics, 2002)

Both surveys included clinical interviews from the DSM-IV that assessed symptoms of mental illness within the last 12 months. Results indicated that more than half of all inmates had a mental health problem.[12] This included 78,800 people in federal prisons (45%), 705,600 in state prisons (56%), and 479,000 in local jails (64%). If we go for the conservative estimate and say that about half of inmates have mental illness, that is still significantly higher than the estimated 17.8% prevalence in the general American population. Rates of substance abuse and dependence were also found to be quite high among inmates, particularly among those with a mental illness. Among inmates in state prison, 74.1% of those who had a mental illness were dependent on or abused alcohol or drugs, compared to 55.6% without a mental illness.

In federal prison, 63.6% of inmates with a mental illness were dependent on or abused drugs or alcohol, compared to 49.5% without a mental illness. The same trend held true for inmates in local jails, with 76.4% of those with a mental illness also living with alcohol or drug abuse/dependency, compared to 53.2% of those who didn't have a mental illness.[13] It's clear that like mental illness, substance abuse disorders are higher among the inmate population than among the general population. It seems to be even more pronounced among inmates struggling with mental illness.

It's important to be careful not to draw conclusions about cause and effect, but the evidence

12   (Bureau of Justice Statistics, US Department of Justice, 2006)
13   (Bureau of Justice Statistics, US Department of Justice, 2006)

suggests that mental illness may make one more susceptible to substance abuse. It also seems that substance abuse and crime tend to occur together. Data collected by the Bureau of Justice Statistics in 2002 and 2004 suggests that about 43% of inmates without a mental illness in state prisons and local jails, along with about 31% in federal prisons, were using drugs or alcohol when they committed their offenses. These numbers are even higher for inmates with mental illness – about 53% of state prison inmates, 54% of local jail inmates, and about 41% of federal prison inmates.

A study examining prevalence of current and lifetime mental illness among inmates in five Connecticut jails found that 32% of inmates met the diagnostic criteria for a current anxiety disorder, 21% for a current mood disorder, and 11.9% for current post-traumatic stress disor-der. This means that those inmates had those disorders while in prison, at the time the data was collected. Lifetime rates of mental illness among the inmates were even higher.[14]

This study excluded inmates who were identified at intake as being acutely mentally ill. The implication of this is that these conditions may be undetected at intake, and therefore inmates may not be getting the treatment they need while serving their time. Despite the high rates of mental illness and substance use among inmates in all three types of correctional facilities (federal prisons, state prisons, and jails), data suggests that most of them do not receive mental health treatment on the inside, and

---

14   (Trestman, Ford, Zhang, & Wiesbrock, 2007)

even fewer receive it in the year prior to their arrest. [15]

Results from a study examining data from two nationally representative surveys found that about 18% of inmates in state and federal prisons were on medication for a mental illness upon admission, but fewer than half of them continued their medication while incarcerated.[16] This indicates a disruption in continuity of care and could be detrimental to the health of the inmate, and to his or her chances of success upon release.

Drugs are often used to manage symptoms of depression, anxiety, bipolar disorder, and posttraumatic stress disorder. They are almost always used to manage severe mental illness like schizophrenia. If people come off their medication when they move into the extremely stressful environment that is prison, they may experience devastating symptoms. In some very serious cases, their behavior may even become dangerous to themselves or to others, as they struggle to deal with threatening situations (real or perceived).

It is essential that people with mental illness who are sentenced to incarceration receive the ongoing treatment and support they need to manage their condition. If our justice system cannot commit to this basic human right, then people with mental illness should not serve time in these facilities. This lack of access to proper mental healthcare in correctional facilities is a serious problem. Prison is no place for someone struggling with a mental illness.

---

15   (Trestman, Ford, Zhang, & Wiesbrock, 2007)
16   (Reingle Gonzalez & Connell, 2014)

If these people are not able to access the treat-ment they need to address their illnesses, how can they be expected to recover? Being incarcerated is a stressful experience for anyone. The fact is that prison is a horrible place. Incarceration often means exposure to violence, poor living conditions, social isolation, feelings of self-loathing, and intense worries about the future. Adjusting to that kind of life is extremely difficult for anyone.

For someone with a mental illness, it might be impossible. These types of conditions are liable to bring about mental health issues for the healthiest person—never mind someone who is already struggling. If a person with a mental illness is sentenced to incarceration and doesn't receive treatment for their illness while serving their time, what are the chances that they are going to be in a good place when they are released? Hint: the chances are very poor.

Forcing people who are mentally ill to serve their time in an environment that will likely make their illness worse, while denying them the treatment they need, is cruel. It also makes it extremely unlikely that they will be ready to successfully transition to life on the outside once they have paid their debt to society.

When someone comes to prison with poor mental health, has their needs are ignored during their sentence, and is then chucked back into the world without support, they don't have much of a chance. With a system like this, there is no wonder that recidivism rates are what they are. This is another example of how the criminal justice system in America is setting offenders up to fail, when they should be helping them rehabilitate and prepare for a new life. It's clear that many inmates with mental illness will have a very difficult incarceration, especially if proper treatment is not made available to them.

It is also safe to assume that the experience will put them at a disadvantage upon being released. Besides the internal suffering and the struggle to take care of their health while dealing with the overwhelming prospect of starting a new life, what other struggles does a freshly released man or woman with mental health issues face? As it turns out, plenty. In the year 2000, 89% of 1558 state correctional facilities reported providing mental health services to inmates.[17]

Just as inmates often do not have access to the healthcare they need while serving their time, once released they continue to struggle. Once release who know how long they may continue to live without treatment and much needed medication. A 2005-2006 study exploring the help-seeking activities of inmates with serious mental illness participating in a reentry pro-gram found that getting access to housing and financial assistance were their top priorities. Specifically, of the 115 program participants who were included in the study, 63% identified housing as one of their top two needs post-release, while 35% identified financial assistance. Even though these participants had serious mental illness, only 12% identified accessing mental health services post release as a top priority.[18] These results do not mean that mental

---

17   (Beck & Maruschak, 2001)
18   (Blank Wilson, 2013)

healthcare is not important for formerly incarcerated reintegrating into society. What it means is that when being released, there are more immediate, pressing concerns that their sur- literally depends on. Deteriorating mental health may threaten their lives, but hunger and exposure do too, in a very tangible way. It is not surprising that most reentry program partici-pants surveyed said that housing is their top priority. They need somewhere to go. How can they focus on getting the mental health treat-ment they need when they are worried about whether they will have somewhere to sleep?

A person's life depends on having shelter and food. Until those needs are met, it is unlikely that a newly released man or woman will be able to focus on anything else. It is truly alarming to realize that although mental illness is so preva-lent among inmates, the barriers to reentry they face are so significant that they are forced to put their health on the back burner. Successful reentry isn't just about getting a job and a safe place to live; it's also about adjusting to a new life and making peace with your past. Without access to mental health resources, these things can be unattainable.

We know that former inmates face substantial barriers to obtaining secure housing and financial assistance, and that these needs are the most pressing. But even when these needs are met, they may struggle to access appropri-ate mental health services upon release. Even people who have never been incarcerated struggle to access mental health services! There are many reasons for this, and they intersect.

One reason people don't access mental health ser-vices is that our society still stigmatizes mental illness.

There tends to be a perception that mental illness is less legitimate or debilitating than physical illness, which is simply not the case. The result is that people are embarrassed and afraid to admit that they are struggling with their mental health and that they need help. Seeking mental health services might be accompanied by feelings of shame or weakness. It might also be accompanied by judgment by one's employer, family, and friends. It's sad to say, but some employers discriminate against employees who are struggling with their mental health. Which is a crime but, yet they continue to do so. If you are victim are a witness of this make sure to document, it and report it.

Because of this, many employees with mental health concerns are afraid to disclose it to their employers. These feelings of fear and shame can be strong enough to prevent people from ever acknowledging their mental health concerns. For this reason, it's very likely that some people struggling with mental illness suffer silently, never seeking the treatment they need.

Former inmates are already dealing with intense levels of stigma because of their criminal records and are especially vulnerable. If a person with a criminal record overcomes the substantial barriers to finding a job, the last thing he or she wants to do is take time off work to go to medical appointments or admit to their employer that they are struggling with a mental illness. Even if the stigma associated with mental illness wasn't so strong, there are still practical barriers to accessing all types of healthcare, including mental healthcare. In the United States, the costs associated with mental healthcare prevent many, especially those with-out insurance, from obtaining the care they need.

There is some evidence to suggest that having public insurance (Medicare or Medicaid) is associated with increased mental health services utilization among people with serious mental illness.[19] This is likely because serious mental illness tends to co-occur with low income, and public insurance would likely be the only way people in these circumstances would be able to afford proper healthcare. Up until recently, many former inmates did not have access to public insurance. In 2013, the expansion of Medicaid under the Affordable Care Act meant that in many states, offenders became eligible for Medicaid once released.

Traditionally, eligibility for Medicaid was reserved for low-income adults with a disability, or who were pregnant. The expansion of Med-icaid that 32 states have elected to participate in removed the pregnant or disabled eligibility criterion, making the insurance available to any non-elderly low-income adult.[20] This was an important step forward for healthcare in the United States. It is important to note, however, that 19 states (including Texas) have opted not to expand their Medicaid programs. Even though the expansion of Medicaid was a beneficial change for former inmates, they still

19   (McAlpine & Mechanic, 2000)
20   (Ollove, 2013)

face significant barriers to accessing healthcare, including mental healthcare.

Just because many of them are now eligible for Medicaid does not mean that once released, they are magically enrolled. There is a strong need for reentry programs that help offenders transition back into society through connect-ing them with community services, including helping them enroll for public health insurance. Applying for Medicaid can be done online, in person, or by mail. Either of these options may be difficult for a former inmate, depending on their literacy, computer literacy, availability of identification documents, access to money, and access to transportation.

Sending a form in the mail or turning up at a public office may sound like a very simple thing, but if someone doesn't have the required documents (for example, birth certificate or proof of income), they are not going to get very far. There are fees associated with obtaining lost identity documents, and when someone is fresh out of prison with no job, they may not have access to those funds. They may not even have access to funds to pay for postage to mail a form! Going to the office in person might prove problematic too if they don't have access to transportation.

In terms of filling out a form online, a newly released man or woman may or may not have access to a computer, and even if they do, they may need help completing the form. This is just one of the many tasks that people just getting released might need help with. It seems like a small thing but making sure they can access public health insurance immediately upon release dramatically increases the chances that they will be able to access timely healthcare. This is one of many reasons that reentry pro-grams that target the unique needs of inmates preparing for release are so important. Transitioning back into society after spending time on the inside is a daunting task that requires ongoing support.

Accessing healthcare, including mental health-care is an essential part of rehabilitation on the inside, and successful reentry to life on the outside. In most cases, those who are formerly incarcerated need help getting started with it, and we need to make sure they are getting that help. It can be easy to categorize inmates and former inmates as criminals. If you have served time, you know what I'm talking about all too well. If you haven't served time, you might be feeling a little uncomfortable right about now. Please remember that the people you might write off as criminals are human beings first.

Yes, they were convicted of a crime, but that doesn't mean they don't deserve human rights. Many people don't stop to consider this, but inmates and former inmates, especially those struggling with mental illness, are some of the most disadvantaged and vulnerable people in our society. How can we treat our most disadvantaged citizens says a lot about the kind of nation we are, we got to do better than this? We have no other choice but to do better.

Chapter Five

Given what we know about the prison experience and the reentry experience that typically follows, we need to focus on developing solutions for change. When I refer to the prison experience, I'm referring to the overcrowded, often dangerous, living conditions; the poor food; the isolation from family and friends; and the limited access to proper healthcare. I'm referring to the constant state of fear that one lives in while incarcerated—in prison, anything can happen on a dime. A riot, an attack, you name it. Things could seem relatively peaceful one minute and turn into a war zone the next. Often, there is no obvious reason for these events.

Being in the wrong place at the wrong time is a perpetual risk, and you learn to never relax, because you never know when something is going to happen. When I refer to the prison expe-rience, I'm referring to the general hopelessness that sets in when you are reduced from an indi-vidual to a number. When you are treated no better than yesterday's trash by (some of) the guards and other inmates and can expect this quality of life to continue for the foreseeable future (in some cases, for years). I'm also talking about the fact that in some prisons, there are no opportunities to engage in anything that could be remotely linked to rehabilitation.

No education, no skills training, no enrichment opportunities. Isn't that supposed to be the point of a non-life sentence? That someone who committed an offence will go to prison, serve their time, rehabilitate, and then return to society having learned their lesson, as a better person? If you're thinking it sounds too good to be true, it's because it is. Here's a reality check: for most people, going to prison does not promote any kind of positive change.

What it does promote is poor mental health, isolation, and low chances of success upon release. This needs to change. When I talk about the reentry experience, I mean the uphill battle that most inmates struggle to fight once they are released. The barriers to finding a safe place to live, the lack of an opportunity to obtain employ-ment and earn income, the lack of access to healthcare, and the unaddressed physical and mental health concerns that go with it.

Not to mention the constant stigma and dis-crimination that former inmates deal with every day. Trying to connect with others is an ongoing struggle, because you constantly have your past hanging over your head, and you never know how a new acquaintance will react. These fears lead some former inmates to isolate themselves from their communities. It also increases the chances that they will reconnect with old friends from their old lifestyle, which might put them at risk for getting involved in criminal activity again.

I've said it before and I'll say it again: the justice system in America is broken. It is supposed to rehabilitate prisoners, but what it really does (in many cases) has put them through hell, and then chuck them back into society without the tools or resources they need to have any kind of chance at success. Yes, some prisons are implementing reentry programs that are doing excellent work, but there is a dire need for a nationwide focus on developing and implementing reentry programs in every prison and jail in America.

Clearly, if the situation is to improve, there is a need for reform on two levels: the day-to-day experience of prisoners, as well as reentry planning. I am a big believer that everybody deserves to be treated with respect, and am firmly against the mistreatment of prison inmates, regardless of conviction. I'm not saying that people should not have to serve their time, but the loss of their freedom is the punishment—they shouldn't be subject to abuse while they are incarcerated.

It is necessary to improve aspects of prisoners' daily lives. This includes things like the quality of the food, access to fresh air and exercise, private bathrooms, visitation privileges, protection from the threat of violence, and access to proper healthcare, including mental healthcare services. As big of an issue as prisoner human rights are, this problem is even larger in scope than that. This flawed system has implications for our communities.

We know that recidivism rates are high, and we can reason that this must be linked to the options available to formerly incarcerated inmates upon release. As discussed earlier, if a person is released from prison with nowhere to go, no job leads, no access to resources to help them find a job, and no access to social assistance, they don't have many choices.

Many times, the only people they got to turn to, if they have anyone at all, are old friends who are still involved in crime. If they don't have access to money, the only way to survive might be to steal, or to sell drugs. If these people were given the resources and tools they need to successfully reintegrate as contributing members of society, it is less likely that they would commit these crimes. And fewer crimes are great for everybody. Fewer crimes mean safer neighborhoods.

Fewer crimes mean fewer people incarcerated, which mean fewer tax dollars spent on prisons, which mean more money to spend on other important things (health, education, etc.). If I can take the liberty of simplifying a complex matter, effective reentry programs are a win-win. We expect people to get out of jail and start new lives as law-abiding citizens, but we make it almost impossible for them to do it. We expect prisons to rehabilitate criminals, when there is no good reason to think that will work. In short, we need an innovative approach.

There is evidence to suggest that participation in specialized reentry programs is associated with reduced recidivism rates.[21] For example, the Connecticut Offender Reentry Program (CORP) was designed to address the needs of serious and violent offenders who have both a metal.

---

21   (Kesten, et al., 2012)

health disorder and a substance use disorder. These inmates typically have complex needs and have a substantial risk of recidivism, likely partly due to inadequate supports.

Another example is the Jail in Reach Project in Harris County, Texas.[22] It is the result of a partnership between Harris County Jail, Health-care for the Homeless-Houston (HHH), and the Mental Health Mental Retardation Authority (MHMRA) of Harris County. It is a health-care based intensive case management program that targets people from the homeless population with a mental illness or substance use disorder who are incarcerated in Harris County Jail. Intensive case management is a model of care characterized by low caseloads, assertive outreach, provision of services in one's own environment, and practical assistance with daily living skills.[23]

The program involved case managers providing in reach services to inmates, defining their needs for post-release, and developing a dis-charge plan. These case managers liaise with community partners to establish linkages and facilitate the transfer of documents relevant to treatment from Harris County Jail to the appropriate service providers so that inmates continue to have access to the services they need post-release.[24] The program operates based on the premise that the County Jail is the largest provider of mental healthcare services in the state of Texas.

---

22   (Healthcare for the Homeless Houston, 2017)
23   (Mueser, Bond, Drake, & Resnick, 1998)
24   (Buck, Brown, & Hickey, 2011)

They estimate that about 25% of county jail inmates have a mental disorder, and that 2400 are taking prescribed psychotropic medication to treat their conditions while incarcerated. Once these inmates are released, it is essential that they continue to have access to medication and mental health services. This is the goal of the program.

A preliminary evaluation of the Jail In reach Project showed that most of the 492 inmates who participated in the program while they were incarcerated were successfully linked to community services post-release.24 Inmates who were released into the care of a case manager (rather than just leaving jail on their own) had particularly high rates of being successfully linked to community services. Furthermore, a comparison of program inmate arrest rates one year prior to program participation to arrest rates one year after program participation showed a 36% decrease.

Some did spend time in jail in the year fol-lowing program participation, but average time spent in jail decreased from 65 days to 42 days, and total number of criminal charges decreased by 56%.24 These results show the importance of discharge planning, and of ensuring inmates have access to proper healthcare in prisons and continue to have access in the community after their release. Linking formerly incarcerated people to community service providers who can provide them with the services they need seems to be linked to reduced recidivism. No program is going to bring recidivism to zero, because there are a multitude of factors involved.

But that isn't the point; the point is to develop programs that will give formerly incarcerated people the tools they need to thrive in their free lives, so they will not resort back to the life of crime. The Northern Kentucky Female Reoffender Program provides intensive case management to help female inmates struggling with mental health/substance use reentry barriers.

Evaluation of this program showed that receiving intensive case management while incarcerated was associated with positive edu-cation outcomes (like earning a GED).[25] It also showed that continuing intensive case manage-ment after release was associated with better employment outcomes, increased participation in mental health/substance use treatment, and a lower risk of committing a new crime. [26] Again, this suggests that there are clear benefits to providing case management to inmates while incarcerated, and to continuing to support them post-release. Take advantage of any education that will better prepare you for the outside.

Having someone to advocate on your behalf can make a dramatic difference when you are released from prison. It can make it easier to land a job and easier to access healthcare, among other things. On the topic of healthcare, in addition to making it easier to get healthcare, having some-one who can encourage you to prioritize yourself, and help you physically get to appointments can also make a significant difference.

Sometimes it can be hard to make sure you're taking care of yourself on top of everything else

---

25   (McDonald & Arlinghaus, 2014)
26   (McDonald & Arlinghaus, 2014)

you got to deal with it as a newly released man or woman. It is good to know that some jails and prisons are working with community partners to try to provide inmates with necessary healthcare services, education opportunities, and discharge planning that they need to have a chance at successful reintegration. These facilities are on the right track, but there are still so many that are not doing their part.

The take away from these examples is that it is possible to successfully run reentry programs, and that they have significant benefits. Providing inmates with resources like education, proper healthcare, and discharge planning is a good thing. What is even better though, is going one step further. It isn't enough to just improve life while in prison and help inmates prepare for release. That is a step in the right direction, but what they also need is for the support to con-tinue once they are back out in the world.

There is evidence to indicate that reentry pro-grams have positive impacts. There is evidence in published peer-reviewed literature, and there is evidence from anecdotes of the people who have lived through it. So why isn't this enough to spark a widespread change? Barriers still exist. Funding is a large one—developing and implementing programs that work require financial and human resources that may not be available. This is where the government, both at the state and federal level, need to step up to the plate and make a change.

As a country, we desperately need more fund-ing to improve prison conditions and to develop and implement reentry programs. Doing this will help inmates transition into life on the outside, with the tools they need to become productive law-abiding citizens. Another barrier to reform is ignorance. The sad truth is that there are a lot of people in our society who are ignorant to these issues.

A lot of people have never been through it, and it's hard for them to grasp just how hard it is. Many of them can't appreciate how flawed the system is, because they don't know the struggles that former inmates face once they get released. Apart from never having been through it, most people just don't spend a lot of time thinking about prison or reentry, because prisons are generally strategically located on the outskirts of cities.

For these reasons, it is so important to educate the public about the realities of imprisonment in America, and the struggles that exist upon reentry. If people don't know about something, if they don't have the facts, then of course they aren't going to care a whole lot about it. Building awareness and promoting education is the key to breaking down ignorance and the apathy that tends to accompany it. This ties into the issue of government funding, too, because ultimately, citizens elect governments, and governments are obligated to pursue avenues that are most important to the majority.

So, if the public doesn't see prison reform as a priority, then it may never become one for the government. It is one thing to be ignorant. It is not a desirable quality, but all of us are ignorant about some things. After all, nobody knows everything, right? We should strive to keep ourselves informed about critical issues affecting our communities and the people in them and share our knowledge about these things when we can. Promoting awareness and sharing educational resources does a lot for reducing ignorance.

But some people are worse than ignorant: they are prejudiced. There are people in our country who believe that prisoners don't deserve fit living conditions. They believe that if a person is convicted of a crime, then they are inferior human beings who don't deserve their basic rights. I disagree with this view more strongly than I can say. People commit crimes for all sorts of rea-sons. Yes, some people who commit crimes are bad people who need to spend the rest of their lives in prison.

But most people who are convicted of crimes do not fall into that category. Many of them were dealing with complex socioeconomic disadvantages that may have been influential in their involvement with crime. Some people are quick to write that off as an excuse, but let me ask you this: What do you think you would do if you were born into poverty? If you were born to a single parent who was struggling with drug addiction? If you didn't know where you would be living next month, or where your next meal was coming from? This is not a good feeling and it is in humane to have go live this way.

What do you think you would do if you lived in an area where you saw crime all the time? If you had to learn to be tough to protect yourself? If coming from that area colored, the way every-one outside of it saw you? If you don't know the answers to these questions, then you are lucky, because you haven't found yourself in these circumstances. But some people have, and some people do. Some people make bad choices that lead to bad circumstances, but some people are born into them.

Maybe you know that one guy who grew up hard, had all the odds against him, but man-aged to turn his life around. That's great for him. But that is one guy. The fact is that social and economic mobility are very difficult to achieve, and most people who are born into poverty stay there. Not because they want to, obviously, but because they have fewer opportunities and face greater barriers than other people do.

So why am I going on about this? Because incarceration disproportionately affects people from low-income families.[27] That means that people from low-income households are more likely to be convicted of crimes and sentenced to time in jail or prison. Why do you think that is? I think that part of the reason is because these people are much more likely than people with middle or high incomes to have to turn to crime to survive. They are more likely to live in areas where they are exposed to crime. They are more likely to be stigmatized by society and treated suspiciously by police (this seems especially true for minorities). They are also more likely to be victims of crime. My point is that you never know what kind of battle someone is fighting, and our society would be a lot kinder and a lot more tolerant if we could suspend judgment and try to understand that the world is not always as simple as want.

27   (Brookings, 2014)

Some people who make very bad mis-takes are still good people who deserve another chance. If you are reading this book because you are a reentry advocate, or because you think you might like to become one, then there are several things you can do to help the cause.

You can contribute financially to community organizations working to help former inmates reintegrate. Better yet, you can volunteer your time. If you can't do either of these things, that's ok. You can educate yourself about the factors associated with crime, what life in jail/prison is like, and the barriers former inmates face. Then you can start a dialogue about it with your friends.

Awareness is the enemy of ignorance, and this small step goes a long way. It is the first step to changing public attitudes about the justice system in America, and that is what needs to happen if we are going to achieve prison reform. If you are currently struggling to reintegrate into society after serving your time, or will be soon, then I wish you strength on your journey – you're going to need it. If you are lucky enough to be part of a reentry program, or to be working with a case manager or some other type of advocate, then I urge you to take advantage of every single opportunity you get through those channels.

I know sometimes that isn't easy, because you're scared, or you don't know what to expect, but this is such a valuable resource to be cap-italized on. If you aren't lucky enough to have someone advocating for you, I urge you to reach out to organizations in your community whose mandate it is to help those struggling to get on their feet. Reentry advocate organizations are best, because they know your unique struggles, but if one is not available, any organization aiming to help disadvantaged people will do. You are likely to find non-judgmental people there, who are educated about the socioeconomic factors that can have such a massive impact on our lives.

Chapter Six

If you're reading this book, it's likely that you've heard the term "mass incarceration" or 'mass imprisonment" tossed around from time to time. If you're not 100% sure what those terms mean, I will take the opportunity to clarify them. Mass incarceration (or mass imprisonment) refers to the fact that America imprisons more people than any other country in the world[28], and that we imprison many more people than we used to.

In the past 40 years, incarceration rates in our country have increased by about 500%, even though crime rates have not.[29] This dramatic increase can mostly be explained by changes in laws and policies. The "war on drugs" that began in the 1980s was and is an important example of how policy changes can affect the justice system. Between the years of 1980 and 2015, the number of people imprisoned for a drug related offence increased by over 1000%. That means there are more than ten times as

---

28   (Walmsley, 2013)
29   (The Sentencing Project, 2017)

many people in prison for drug-related offenses as of 2015 than there were in 1980.

The result is that prisons are overcrowded, and taxpayers are overburdened by the costs associated with supporting such a huge prison population. Reintegrating into society after serving a prison sentence is extremely challenging for all the reasons we've discussed. But it's also difficult because you are in a culture that pro-motes imprisonment before prevention. You and I both know because of your record, you will be judged more harshly.

If you ever have a run -in with the law again You're past will be used against you. It is likely that this contributes to high recidivism rates. The barriers to going legit put former inmates in an inconvenient situation, and sometimes they turn to criminal activity. Of course, at this point, they have at least one "prior", so the justice system is going to be very hard on them if they are arrested again. It is quite likely that they will receive a harsh sentence and return to prison. It's a vicious cycle.

The "tough on crime" stance of the US jus-tice system disproportionately affects minorities and people of low socioeconomic status. This is mostly because, as discussed in the last chapter, these people tend to face the most significant barriers to meeting their basic needs and are thus more likely to resort to something that will get them in trouble with the law.

In the case of minorities (particularly black men and men of middle eastern descent), some would say that police are more suspicious of them, and that the law is harder on them.

Racism in law enforcement is an important topic that I haven't said much about. This isn't because I don't think it's important, but because it is so large in scope, and such a multi-layered problem, that I can't do it justice in a book of this length. I will say that racism is alive and well in America, and that it plays an active role in our justice system.

If we want to see crime rates go down, investing money in prevention, rather than punishment, might be the answer. I'm not trying to convince you that all crimes are committed because people are desperate, but some certainly are. I'm willing to bet that if we had fewer people in our country living in poverty, we would have fewer crimes being committed. We need to invest in social housing programs, so that people have safe places to live.

We need to invest in education, so that adults without high school diplomas can earn them, and so that children from low-income neigh-borhoods are not forced to go to inferior schools. We need to invest in job skills training programs, so that unemployed people can have a chance at finding work. We need to ensure that our most vulnerable people have access to afford-able healthcare. We need to take food security seriously, so that people in our country are not left wondering how they will get their next meal.

If our country could be a little less tough on crime and a little tougher on poverty, we might see some positive changes. Even though we are living in the era of mass incarceration, we know that most people incarcerated today will even-tually be released. Therefore, much of this book has been focused on reentry; the barriers that come with it, and strategies for dealing with them. The reality is that every day hundreds of Americans are leaving prison or jail and begin-ning the struggle of reintegrating into a society that may not welcome them.

In most cases, our system does not provide them with the tools and resources they need to be successful in their new lives. In short, our system sets them up to fail. The situation is dire, but there are things we can do at a community level to make changes. Nobody can single-hand-edly fix our justice system or the barriers former inmates face in society. However, each of us can do something to help. The number one thing any member of the public can do is try to educate yourself about the issues and try to engage in positive discourse with other people.

Education and awareness are the enemies of ignorance, and ignorance is at the core of apathy, and at the core of prejudice. You can also try your best to give former inmates the benefit of the doubt. The truth is, you don't know why they did what they did. They have already been judged for their crime and paid their debt to society. So, try not to judge them again. Try not to make them keep paying for their mistake. Instead, let them have a second chance and treat them as you would any other human being.

If you're in the privileged position of being a business owner, or a hiring manager, I urge you not to dismiss the applicant with the criminal record based on that alone. Consider what they could offer your organization, and how important a role you could play in giving a disadvantaged person a chance to prove themselves. The same goes for a landlord or a property manager. If you can, give that applicant a chance. Get your deposit and take a risk. Maybe it won't work out, same as any tenant, but maybe it will. You have no idea the difference having safe and secure housing makes to someone struggling to get on their feet after being released from prison or jail.

Be that person who is willing give someone a fair chance. If you're the friend or family member of someone just released, or someone who will soon be released, your role is so important. Your loved one is going through something extremely difficult. They are facing significant barriers in their external environments, but what they might not be saying is that they are likely experiencing internal struggles, too. They are likely feeling ashamed of having been in prison and scared about what their lives will be like now.

These feelings might be mixed in with feelings of hope for the future, or anger at the system, or distrust of people in general. Every individual is different, so it's hard to predict exactly what someone is going to be feeling, and chances are, they will have conflicting emotions that they might struggle to make sense of sometimes, this can cause a person to withdraw. If you are the friend or family member of someone going through this, it is important to be supportive and non- judgmental. Let them know that you are there for them, that you accept them, and that they won't be alone in this.

If they resist spending time with you and seem to be self-isolating, you want to respect their privacy but try to keep in contact, so they know you're serious about being there. There are sup-port groups available for people in your position. Having a family member or close friend go to prison can be very stressful, and many people in that position find support and comfort by connecting with other people going through the same thing.

If you're part of such a group, try to learn from the experience of others. You might be struggling with some negative feelings yourself—maybe you're angry or resentful towards the person in your life who went away to prison. Those feel-ings are normal, and it might help to talk about it with a support group, or with a counselor in

a   one-on-one setting. It's very important that you continue to take care of your own mental health—you can't help your loved one if you're unwell yourself. Encourage your friend or family member who is newly released to take care of their health, as well. If need be, help them arrange appointments, and if you can, offer to drive them and accompany them.

If you suspect that their mental health is so bad that they might be a danger to themselves, or to others then contact professional help immediately. Standing by someone's side as they attempt to adjust to life on the outside is not easy, just as the task they are facing is not. Even if they may not say it now, your support is going to make an enormous difference in your friend or family member's life. I hope you won't give up on them. Maybe you don't have anyone close to you who is struggling with incarceration or reentry, but you care about the cause. That's wonderful!

Society needs more people like you to step up as reentry advocates. Don't worry, that doesn't mean you need to go all in. Just do what you can, because every little bit helps. Maybe you can afford to donate a few dollars to a local advocacy group? That's great! I'd encourage you do a bit of research, so you know your hard-earned money is supporting a program doing work you believe in. If you can't afford to contribute financially, that's ok.

There are lots of other ways you can help. Many programs might be seeking donations of slightly used household items or clothing to help newly released people get started. Maybe you have something at home that you're not using that might be able to help someone out. Many programs offering supports for former inmates rely on government funding to hire staff, and we know that's often scarce. The result is that they may need volunteers to help with some of their work. Volunteering even a couple of hours of your time can make a significant difference.

Maybe you'd like to work directly with pro-gram participants, or maybe you wouldn't. Either option is fine. Just tell the organization what you're comfortable with and ask how you can help. Trust me, they will be grateful! Don't forget, everyone has a voice. Maybe you don't think yours will make a difference, but you're wrong. Maybe you have thought about some of these same things. If you like me maybe you've questioned how our current system can possibly promote rehabilitation.

Maybe you wish things were different. Well, maybe they can be. We are blessed to live in a democratic country, and our governments are elected by us to work for us. So, voice your concerns to your municipal, state, and federal representatives. Call or email the person you elected to represent you, and let your voice be heard. Maybe you'll dismiss this advice, because what is one phone call going to do?

Well, one phone call isn't much, but if everyone who decided not to bother because it wouldn't make a difference, then noting would get done. However, if you and others decided to make that call, we could then give our government something to think about. If you are currently incarcerated, you might have started to think about what will happen after you are released. You might be scared about what your future will look like. I'm not going to lie: it's not going to be easy. You probably already know the type of challenges you are going to face. If you're lucky enough to be participating in a reentry program at your facility, my best advice is to get absolutely everything you can from it.

It would be wise to seize any education or vocational training opportunities that comes your way. Because at the end of the day it will help you in the future It will make it easier for you when you get released and are looking for work. If you have the option of working with a case manager, then do it. Basically, take advantage of any and every possible opportunity for self-improvement or preparation because you are going to need it. When you get out, try your best to connect with a reentry advocacy group as soon as you can.

Hopefully, they will be able to help you join a support group. I know you will be overwhelmed with everything on your plate during this diffi-cult time but having support during this time is crucial. If you have a relationship with a case manager who wants to stay in touch, make sure you do. Your case manager can help you take care of essential things like getting identification documents in order, applying for health insurance, securing safe housing, and looking for a job.

If you don't have anyone like that in your corner, people at the reentry advocacy group can likely help. If you are lucky enough to have family and friends waiting for you, let them help you. Sometimes this can be tough. Although they mean well, they likely can't really relate to what you're going through. But it is important to have people in your life and to not isolate yourself. That's one reason why it's valuable to join a support group for former inmates—It helps to talk to people who know your struggle. Having people in your life who have been through what you have been through is a reliable source of inspiration and guidance.

But your friends and family who may not necessarily "get it" are valuable too, and it important to stay connected to them. The road ahead is going to be rough, but the more prepared you are, the better your chances will be. Never give up on yourself, and never stop believing that you deserve a second chance. If you've recently been released for prison, you might be struggling. I know I did. Maybe you haven't had luck finding housing, and you're staying in a shelter. Maybe you're not sure where you'll be living next week, or how you'll get money to pay.

It's possible that you haven't been able to deal with important tasks like applying for health insurance or seeing a doctor. You might be struggling with physical or mental health issues. I know you're likely dealing with stigma and shame, and you might be losing hope. If you have someone advocating for you, like a case manager, someone from a reentry program, or a parole officer, then that's a very positive thing. Make sure you take their advice and let them help you to the best of their abilities. If you are one of the many who are not lucky enough to have someone, trust me, you aren't alone. It is essential that you connect with a group or pro-gram that can help you get on your feet. Most communities will have something like this.

A reentry program or a group that works specifically with former inmates is ideal, because they are used to helping people dealing with the same challenges you are. If there isn't a resource like this in your community, don't despair, because there is most likely some group, or groups, who work with disadvantaged people who need a helping hand getting back on their feet after tough times. If you can get to a computer, or get your hands on a phone book, you can find this information. If you need help accessing either of these things, and don't have a friend or family member to help, try the local library. Along with going to prison in the first place, trying to reintegrate into society is probably one of the most challenging things you will ever do.

I know the barriers, the disappointments, and the feeling that it is never going to get better. I won't lie and tell you there is a magical solution, but I can say that it does get better with time, you just got to keep fighting. Yes, it will be a challenge; it's an uphill battle, and sometimes you might think that you won't make it. You basically have two choices ahead of you. You can go back to your old ways and can end up back in prison. You can keep fighting, every single day, to rebuild your life. It's not an easy choice.

Many formerly incarcerated people end up going back for a variety of reasons, and I don't judge them for it. But that doesn't have to be you. This freedom, this second chance at life, is yours. You earned it. You are going to meet people who don't think you deserve it, who will treat you as though you're not worthy, but you can't let them in your head. Try your best to surround yourself with good people, supportive people, or even just one person. If you don't have anyone in your life like that, go out into the community and try to make some connections. It's not easy, but there are decent people out there who will be willing to look past your mistake.

At the end of the day, we all make mistakes. Some mistakes are bigger than others, and some big mistakes land us in prison. One of the hardest things in the world is forgiving your-self for a terrible mistake. You might not think you deserve it, but I do. You cannot change the past. It's done, and it's gone and dwelling on it will not change it. But you can change both your present and your future today. Make peace with your past mistakes and decide what kind of person you want to be going forward.

Every day when you wake up, try to be that person. If you fail one day, try again tomorrow.

When you decide who you want to be, act like that person, every day and eventually you will become him or her. That's the secret to change. Some time you got to fake it until you make it. Remember, you've already survived prison. That wasn't for nothing. If you can do that, you can do anything. You likely had to do some tough things to come out of there in one piece, and you're made of stronger stuff than you think.

Have faith in yourself; some days you might be the only one that does. You are worthy. You do deserve a second chance. You've earned your freedom, and you have the rest of your life ahead of you. What will you do with it? Don't let your past haunt you for the rest of your life. Today is the day you be the change, now that you have a second chance what will you do with it. Don't let the system keep you from being somebody. Get over your wrongs you've made in the past and move forward. Through God anything is possible, look at me no one would have ever though I would be the author of my own book. God is good all the time. Let each day be used in a positive way to help pave the way for the next person returning home after release.

Those who are closet to the problem are closet to the solution, but furthest from resources and power

-JustLeadrshipUSA-

A Letter from the Author

Speaking as a black man, for me my encounter leaving prison was rocky. No one would give me a chance to prove myself, I know the choices I made in the past were wrong. However, I don't feel like I should have to relive my past over and over. Being black and having the label of *convicted felon* is hard. No one want to give you a chance; it's one of those things where you will always have to fight and prove yourself. That's why I tell you this— always stay focused and fight for what you need and never give up no matter how hard things get.

At the end of the day it's better to struggle as a free man; then it's to struggle as a caged man. When I walked out of prison in 2004, I knew that if I could help it I would never return. Yes, when you first get out things will be rocky. But as the time go by things will get better. As a formerly incarcerated individual, it's one of things where you got to want to change. Yes, no doubt there are going to be some roadblocks ahead of you. But don't let those roadblocks detour you from changing. In life, we take many risks, so why not take a risk in seeking a change. Deep down nobody wants to be incarcerated, so prepare yourself to never go back.

Always remember that nothing good comes easy. You got to be willing to humble yourself regardless what others thank or say. When it comes down to it, you can only live your own life. Nobody else can live for you, so trust in yourself and do what is right for you. It's up to you to stay focused and out of trouble, because at the end of the day nobody got you like you got yourself. So many formerly incarcerated people want to do right, yet they return to that old environment and pickup their old habits.

If you really want to change you can't go back to your old ways. Insanity is to do the something repeatedly while expecting a different result. If you truly want to change start hanging with a different crowd. Hanging around people who are doing positive things will make you want to do positive things. Each year, we see new laws enacted to keep us down, we continue to see barriers placed over us, yet we do nothing about it. We got to start letting our voice be heard. Get out and do right and fight for your second chance. Getting out and going back to your old ways, will set you up to fail all over again. Doing positive things after your release will keep you free. It's not hard to do good. You just got to want to do good. I don't know how many times I must say it.

Only you can keep yourself out of trouble. Having a support system can keep you on the right track. But it's still up to you to do right.

At some point in time you got to look out for yourself, that start before you're released from custody. At the end of the day you must prepare yourself to do right. It's one of those things where you need the mindset that you going to do right. Start by educating yourself before you return home. Taking up a trade and gain real world knowledge while you have time. Take advantage of every opportunity that will make you a better person once released. For myself, I took advantage of everything I could. I spent most my time in the law library studying the law.

So that way, I could be more aware of the jus-tice system operated. I educated myself on the law and on how politics operated as well. So, when I got out I took classes and earned my Associate degree as a Paralegal. As a black man who has overcome the odds, I see myself as a testimony. Black people are being incarcerated at a higher rate than any other race. Part of that is being ignorant to the law and being uneducated. When a person has a better understanding of the law, the outcome is always different. We need to start being our own bosses, we need to stop making these companies richer, we need to educate ourselves on how to make money for ourselves.

When I say make money for ourselves that don't mean selling drugs. I'm referring to owning busi-nesses, being an entrepreneur, and investing in your own franchises. Why continue to make the next man richer when you can be rich. We would rather work ourselves to the bone for another man's glory. While they are getting richer, we are struggling. We got to start doing better, we got to start exposing our mind to something new. To be successful in life, you must decrease the odds of being a failure. Just like in football if a player is not producing well you go and make a change. You must make a change in your life if you want to see different results.

Everyone knows that success is based on prob-abilities and odds. No two people are alike, and not everybody has the same playing field. Today, more than ever, the odds are against those leaving prison. We know the barriers that are set before us are designed so we can fail. The prison system is designed to make money off us, so why would they want to design a system to work in our favor. We are the ones who are keeping them in business and making them richer. We need to do better and start working toward putting those money-making machines out of business.

Many of us have made many bad choices that we wish we could take back. But we can't, and we shouldn't dwell on the past. But we can make a better future if we try. Remember that every successful person has failed at something. The one thing they did do was learn from their fail-ures. Our bad choices can become our strength to do better. Staying focus and believing in our-selves goes along ways. When you feel down and alone pray and asked God to give you the strength to continue down the right path.

References

Beck, A. J., & Maruschak, L. M. (2001, July). Mental health treatment in state prisons, 2000. Burau of Justice Statistics Special Report: https://static.prisonpolicy.org/scans/bjs/mhtsp00.pdf Blank Wilson, A. (2013).

How People with Serious Mental Illness Seek Help After Leaving Jail. Qualitative Health Research, 23 (12), 1575.

Brookings. (2014, April 28). Brookings.edu. Retrieved June 17, 2017 from the unequal burden of crime and incarceration on Ameri-ca's poor: https://www.brookings.edu/blog/ up-front/2014/04/28/the-unequalbur-den-of-crime-and-incarceration-on-ameri-cas-poor/

Buck, D. S., Brown, C. A., & Hickey, J. S. (2011). The Jail In reach Project: linking home-less inmates who have mental illness with community health services. Psychiatric Services, 62 (2), 120-122.

Bureau of Justice Statistics. (2004). Data Collection: Survey of Inmates in State Correctional Facilities (SISCF). Retrieved June 6, 2017 from Bueau of Justice Statistics: https://www.bjs.gov/index.cfm?ty=dcdetail&iid=275

Bureau of Justice Statistics. (2002). Data Collection: Survey of Inmates In Local Jails (SILJ). Retrieved June 6, 2017 from Bureau of

Justice Statistics: https://www.bjs.gov/index.cfm?ty=dcdetail&iid=274

Bureau of Justice Statistics, US Department of Justice. (2006, December 14). Bureau of Jus-tice Statistics Special Report: Mental Health problems of Prison and Jail Inmates. Retrieved June 5, 2017 from Bureau of Justice Statistics: https://www.bjs.gov/content/pub/pdf/mhppji.pdf

Carson, E. A., & Anderson, E. (2016, December 29). Prisoners In 2015. Retrieved June 6, 2017 from Bureau of Justice Statistics: https://www.bjs.gov/index.cfm?ty=pbdetail&iid=5869

Center for Behavioral Health Statistics and Quality. (2016). Key Substance Use and Mental Health Indicators in the United States: Results from the 2015 National Survey on Drug Use and

Health. Retrieved June 5, 2017 from Substance Abuse and Mental Health Services

Administration: http://www.samhsa.gov/data/

Healthcare for the Homeless Houston. (2017). Jail Inreach Project. From Healthcare for the Homeless Houston:

https://www.homeless-healthcare.org/jail-in-reach-project-hw/ Ill-equipped: U.S. prisons and offenders with mental illness.

(2003, October 21). From Human Rights Watch: https://www.hrw.org/ r e p o r t / 2 0 0 3 / 1 0 / 2 1 / i l l - e q u i p p e d / us-prisons-andoffenders-mental-illness

Kesten, K. L., Leavitt-Smith, E., Rau, D. R., Shelton, D., Zhang, W., Wagner, J., et al. (2012). Recidivism Rates Among Mentally Ill Inmates: Impact of the Connecticut Offender Reentry Program. Journal of Correctional HealthCare, 18 (1), 20-28.

McAlpine, D. D., & Mechanic, D. (2000). Utilization of specialty mental health care among persons with severe mental illness: the roles of demographics, need, insurance, and risk. Health Serv Res, 35 (1), 277-292. McCarty, M., Falk, G., Aussenberg, R. A., & Carpenter, D. H. (2016). Drug Testing and Crime-Related Restrictions in TANF, SNAP, & Housing Assistance. Congregational

Research Service Report.

McDonald, D., & Arlinghaus, S. L. (2014). The Role of Intensive Case Management Services in Reentry: The Northern Kentucky Female Offender Reentry Project. Women and Criminal Justice, 24 (3), 229-251.

Mueser, K. T., Bond, G. R., Drake, R. E., & Resnick, S. G. (1998) . Models of community care for severe mental illness: A review of reserach on case management. . Schizophrenia Bulletin, 24 (1).

Ollove, M. (2013, April 20). Ex-felons to get health coverage via Affordable Care Ac. From AJC.com: http://www.ajc.com/news/national/felons-get-health-coverage-viaaffordable-care-act/NK1jLFJT4RewM4lzkE7xnI/

Prins, S. J. (2014). The prevalence of Mental Illnesses in US state prisons: a systematic review. Psychiatr Serv. 65(7), 862-872.

Reingle Gonzalez, J. M., & Connell, N. (2014). Mental Health of Prisoners: Identifying Barriers to Mental Health Treatment and Medication Continuity. Am J Public Health, 104 (12), 2328-2333.

The Sentencing Project. (2017, June 19). Criminal Justice Facts. From The Sentencing

Project: http://www.sentencingproject.org/criminal-justice-facts/

Trestman, R. L., Ford, J., Zhang, W., & Wiesbrock. (2007). Current and Lifetime Psychiatric Illness Among Inmates Not Identified as Acutely Mentally Ill at Intake in Connecticut's Jails. Journal of the American Academy of Psychiatry and the Law, 35(4), 490-500.

U.S. Department of Housing and Urban Development. (2017, June 19). Fair Housing and Equal Opportunity. From HUD.gov:

https://portal.hud.gov/hudportal/HUD?src=/program_ offices/fair_housin g_ equal_opp

Walmsley, R. (2013). World Prison Population List (tenth edition). From International Centre for Prison Studies:

http://www.prisonstudies.org/sites/default/files/resources/downloads/wppl_10.pdf.

About the Author

Michael A. Davis is a formerly incarcerated individual. He was a Paralegal with Texas Civil Rights Project. Mr. Davis as holds an undergraduate degree in Paralegal. Michael is currently an advocate with The Reentry Advocacy Project and a sustaing member at Grassroots Leadership in Austin, Texas. He is also a Guardian of Liberty at ACLU of Texas. In 2013 Michael became the first in his family to graduate college. In 2016 Mr. Davis completed JLUSA's Emerging Leadership training, an organization that is known for its closerikers campaign. Michael is currently studying for a bachelor's degree in General Studies and Sociology. He believes that we need a more just system based on fairness, equality and equity, for people can change when given the right tools. Those who are closes to the problem are closets to the solution.

Published by
Beyond the Gates Publishing Co.

The Road to Reentry/ edited by Chris Dirusso

ISBN-13: 978-1717813336
ISBN-10: 171781333X

Printed in the United States of America